POETRY BIRMINGHAM

POETRY BIRMINGHAM
Literary Journal

Winter 2019 — Issue Two

EDITOR

Naush Sabah

VERSE FIRST PRODUCTIONS LTD.
BIRMINGHAM

POETRY BIRMINGHAM
Literary Journal

VerseFirst Productions Ltd, Birmingham
www.VerseFirst.org
© 2019 all individual authors
All rights reserved. Published 2019

Typeset & Design: Suna Afshan, Adrian B. Earle and Naush Sabah
Co-editor: Suna Afshan
Editorial Assistant: Olivia Hodgson

ISSN 2633-0822
ISBN 9781713264033

COVER IMAGE

The Holy Family, 1682
By Benedetto Gennari the Younger
Photo by Birmingham Museums Trust, licensed under Creative Commons CC0

Birmingham
Museums

SUBMISSIONS

For our guidelines visit www.poetrybirmingham.com

Submission windows:
1st to 31st March
1st to 30th June
1st to 30th September
1st to 31st December

After one has abandoned a belief in god, poetry is that
essence which takes its place as life's redemption.

'Adagia', Wallace Stevens

                    Never flinch,
But still, unscrupulously epic, catch
Upon a burning lava of a song,
The full-veined, heaving, double-breasted Age:
That, when the next shall come, the men of that
May touch the impress with reverent hand, and say
'Behold,—behold the paps we all have sucked!
That bosom seems to beat still, or at least
It sets ours beating. This is living art,
Which thus presents, and thus records true life.'

                    'Aurora Leigh', Elizabeth Barrett Browning

Until I felt it at last   the rush of squall thrilling my wing
            and I knew my voice
was no longer words but song   black upon black.

I raised my throat to the wind
                    and this is what I sang . . .

                                        'Bird', Liz Berry

CONTENTS

EDITORIAL

Naush Sabah

Soundtrack: *As-Salat Al-Mashishiyya*, Abdas-Salaam ibn Mashish

> Were it not for the power of convention in which, by a sort of mutual cancellation of errors, the more practical and normal conceptions are enshrined, the imagination would carry men wholly away . . .
>
> *Interpretations of Poetry and Religion*, George Santayana

I have been thinking about A. S. Byatt's essay on storytelling: 'Narration is as much a part of human nature as breath and the circulation of the blood', she wrote in 1999. At the close of this decade, I find myself in a narrative crisis and wondering how that might alter my nature. When some foundational narrative in our lives suddenly collapses, the heart pumps harder, breath becomes shallower and faster and we find ourselves no longer able to suspend disbelief. We're forced instead to defer to our senses and perceptions, and to how our rational faculties conceptualise them. The imagination is left sullenly aside until it can reconvene with reason and construct a new narrative.

Shahrazad's stories kept her alive and, as Byatt argues, that is more than the central conceit of a frame story: it is a fundamental truth about how we function. We build our lives, our communities, our civilizations upon the narratives we weave and choose to believe together, and often we tear them down by pulling at those narrative threads. We retell the same stories over and again to give sense to our seasons, or to console ourselves when we're cornered. Like the sacred—impossible—story of a virgin single mother who withdraws to a remote place to give birth utterly alone, clinging to a date palm in the throes of labour, wishing she were dead, until a stream springs up beneath her and ripe dates fall from above, and her new-born boy speaks to defend her honour.

I wonder how distorted this story seems to some of our readers, as it breaks the water's surface and is refracted; baptised into a newer faith. Powerful stories transform according to need as they pass through the ages and through differing traditions and interpretive lenses: a man can be God's own son, a prophet, a saviour, or a reason for the heads of heretics to be lopped off. He can move armies or move men to tears. In this issue's opening poem, the very same people who 'built homes in the belfry' eventually 'christened it in flames'. When the narrative breaks and congregations disappear leaving 'pages dotted with mould', somehow the stories still find their way back to us with the endless 'promise of razed ground'.

Impossible stories can be the most enchanting of all, since—in the words of Colin Falck—the 'mythic mode of consciousness is a vision of reality . . . a form of integrated perceptual awareness which unites "fact" and "explanation"'. It seems counterintuitive at its surface, that the desire for truth compels us to invest so completely in fictions, and often in fantastical fictions, which in turn create our reality; from the way a single individual loves and lives, to how theology might shape the laws of a whole nation, or how a culture might shape the parameters of acceptable behaviour within it. But somehow, mythological cosmic narratives accentuate deeper human truths and needs. We find spiritual transcendence in the fictive truths that myth alerts our consciousness to. These fictive truths at the core of religious traditions are what keep them relevant, and this human need is what keeps them alive in a post-nihilistic era. God, at least, has an afterlife. The Gardener remains in 'the lovely, empty garden'.

The poems in this issue of the journal are so firmly earthed that they are 'stuck in rutted clay'. This is a good place to be at a time when the Poet Laureate rightly says, 'nature has very much come back into the centre of what poetry can, and should, be dealing with'. And yet it deals also in the cosmos 'beyond it . . . and infinite black', it engages still with the 'wormholes and paradox' of being alive in the archaeological sites that are the cities and the world we live in. It sweeps in scale, from the 'bounding heart' of a delicate bird held in the hand to 'downed fences [and] hung parliaments'. Amidst loss and death and decay, there is nonetheless wonder and countless reasons to say 'Hallelujah'.

'Render unto Caesar the things that are Caesar's and render unto God the things that are God's'. Pithy prophetic sayings sit somewhere close to the realm of poetry in that they strike the mind like a match, with a similar sense of unifying completeness that a good poem can, whilst simultaneously sparking new lines of thought, new layers of meaning. That line, like any, can be turned through interpretation and perhaps none are better at exegesis to their own ends than the self-proclaimed men of God. For them, all things are God's, even Caesar, and so Caesar must be rendered to God (and God's mind can only be known through them). In that way, Christo-Islamic religious traditions have tended to claim dominion over all things within their reach.

The purview of poetry is just as all-encompassing. But what seems a weapon in the hands of religion, is a far gentler instrument in the hands of poetry. Rendering unto poetry the things that are poetry's opens it—our favoured imaginative mode of explaining and knowing reality—to an endless expanse of material for renewed mythologies and renewed narratives. 'The only religious scriptures we shall need . . . will be the poetry or literature to which our culture gives us access' asserts Falck, echoing Matthew Arnold. That idea holds no less hope and promise than a miracle baby born to a virgin mother.

St Michael on the Mount Without

Shattered marble blankets the nave, remains
of funerary monuments long lost
to the figures commemorated on the walls.
Shard of cherub here, sliver of angel there.

Above, weathered beams frame the sky.
Chill air rises through gaps in the floor
from graves bubbling below
releasing spectral vapours into air.

Prayer books sit opened on the altar,
pages dotted with mould. At the base
a kneeling pad rots among rusted candlesticks.
Broken pews are seamed with moss and guano.

The church shut when it lost its congregation,
mislaid them like a set of keys, stood empty
until squatters moved in, built homes in the belfry,
christened it in flames when the city kicked them out.

FIONA LARKIN

Burying the Flowerbed

Once it flourished, spilling out
yellow roses, trailing

vinca, overlaid the clay
with plug-in scents

but the gardener's gone. With him
the love for shoot and thorn.

In a relic haven, growth
is attack. The earth takes back.

Snap off. Hard prune.
What survives is chickweed, nettle.

A bud is choked
by weed-proof membrane.

Scattering of chipped slate.
Jesus, what does that

remind you of?
The lovely, empty garden.

FRANCES BOYLE

Drowning Marzanna

Blue-black vibrations, worn-out moon
wanes. Two fish
                    —no there's a third
—whiskery fish bump against logs,
the abstract shame that surfaces

in memory, a shape filled by twisting
vines that grow along your nerve
endings as a bounty of zucchini spreads
in your frame.
                    You check
your phone the way you used to smoke:
to distract, to pull you away from intensity
or boredom. A morning of dawn-treading,

yawning noons after sleepwalking, the jar
empties, the jar will refill, and a courgette
seems to be a cucumber after all
when you reach for it in the crisper.

The sturgeon bright, the salmon bright,
the way you look tonight in the bathing
moon realigns your face to the active crime
of not knowing.

                    If the shell you touch
is too hard to drink from, scoop up
the calm, the beautiful, place gladiolas
on the burning effigy, poppies to fill

her arms. Scraps of red, and hairy stems
will mark her whelming.
                    You shift
from inattention to focus, a ghostly habit
grasping vines that float on your palms,
rock the lilipad upon the waves, yellow
fish, orange fish, invisible blue in water.

Rebecca Gethin

Holding the Night

I bring it close, one hand under
the belly and one over the wings,
body all feather and skeleton.
Fingertips answer its bounding heart
as if together they created vibrato.

It weighs almost nothing:
a ribcage enclosing
the inner life,
air between wing coverts
silks rubbing.

With one wrong squeeze
it might shatter into birds.
I could fall into the gaping beak
disappear into the pink gullet.
Catchlights of star in the pupils.

The moon has marked
its name on wing and tail.
I never knew that flight is a living thing,
that only by being so light
can it fly so far and carry the dark.

LORRAINE CAREY

Snowfall

Hedgehogs, voles and shrews
while away winter in subnivean slumber.
Above ground, a hungry dog creeps
around vulpine-like on fresh snow,
chasing rabbit scent,
his pace slowed by the deep, packed drifts.

The rubbery pads of his paws
sift and circle the patch.
Evening creeps in as December light
fades, snatches the day.
Children familiar with roadside slush,
acrid smog and fleeting play in parks,
roam and roll down hills, their coats
layered white and their laughter
a muffled echo underground.
Parents stand rooted,
acknowledge an absence of words,
the silence of snow.

ALISON BRACKENBURY

The Final Firework, New Year's Eve

When it reached sky
each single flare
flowered, fell white.

Is that how you weaved, wanderer,
from light to light?

GREGORY LEADBETTER

Solstice, Midwinter

Now the sun is the shining stone of a moon
cool on the skin and film of the eye.

It breathes the earth to mist as light
and gives the skull its star to hold.

Laura Wainwright

Noctua*

A laundry huff of air
and then a weight kneading my shoulder,
testing a left nest.

An owl has shaken me
from a long wakefulness;
her wing sweeps my ear.

I am floored, but follow the track
with the assurance of a falconer.

Trees are lithographs in the hollowing light.
Last week's snow is peeling on the hills like old paint.

What has to die tonight?

When, with ungainly grace,
the owl has gone, brief as a flower,
I scan the needled taupe.

I miss her painfully, like birdsong.
Though she left me a capsule of odd bones.

---

* Latin for 'night owl', and the name of a constellation that is no longer recognised by astronomers.

Upcycling

that old barstool he balanced on for painting,
its heavy oak hatched and spattered,
its legs wobbly as scotch,
I thought of penny-farthings pedalled
uphill by faded, sped-up men.
I slathered it with turpentine, watched, light-headed,
the rainbow years distil and widen
like pupils in the dark, then weep and muddy:
the thawing permafrost of homemaking.
Then, with every scrape of sharpened metal,
the grain returned, in wood-cut waves and cirrus clouds,
and on the sanded seat, varnished to flawed walnut,
I stood a photograph, a fossil

JAY WHITTAKER

Birmingham, Again

Between Smallbrook Queensway and Hill Street
a sinkhole opened.
                    I plunged,
aching to tell a dead woman
how the city reincarnated
multiple times since we left;
                    how it melts down,
reforms into the shape it needs now.
Cranes, crossing cranes.

From a bedroom on the 26th floor
I look down on Victorian civic pride,
pubs tiny as bugs, crouching between towers.
                    Only I lived to remember
our shared history of this city
how we burst out brash
onto last century's vision for these streets,
where neon livened the grubbiest sign.
Always crossed cranes.

The brutalist collarbone still stands
its mould-laced concrete surely marked
for demolition. Each time
this city builds higher, masking
the promise of razed ground.

MATTHEW STEWART

Ordnance Survey

Musty, coffee-cup-stained and frayed
at the folds, your map used to span
the kitchen table while you schemed
a circular walk. Its dead ends

and zig-zag footpaths challenge me
to find a route I've never tried,
to remember all our old ones
and build on those stains, cup by cup.

JEN STEWART FUESTON

Gallery

if you aren't happy   no one can tell
here is the place to imagine

what it might be like to be adored
gather glass smooth as stone   mineraled rare

earth   pixel stitches   certain angles
of bone   foreheads unworried as angels

what is it again that women are loved for?   all this
time and I still don't know   perfection

makes me want to show you the tear   in my dress
in my belly   my adornments of shrapnel

try it on   the gaze   that calculates
it's clear-eyed   like water in the bucket

where they shuck pearls   out of their shells
bare   ly   a shimmer worth wearing

the nacre wound   a mirage
where what remains   unkempt

Going Light

Sometimes you want to knit a net
to catch your own heart in.
So here is the wheat field,
and the range, white and blue,
the shape of all my memories.

This autumn carries on and on.
Sunshine makes crisp lace of leaves
the slightest breeze will end.
I am the last leaf hanging on.

Singing in the going light,
I drive past the sugar mill,
its sweet towers empty, envy
trains passing through the trackyards
on their way to somewhere else.

I become a falconer of a heart
that strays like moonlight through
the waving wheat. Or like a river
everywhere out of its banks.

Across the table from a lonely friend
I want to take her by the hand and tell her,
even everyone who's loved is also still
waiting for love. There is no other
now. You might as well belong.

Remember embryology—
the stomach's formed
before the mouth,
which I take to mean,
our hungers all arrive
before our naming them.

Zoe Brooks

The Rabbit

He must strip himself of gentleness,
peel it off
and, reaching in, pull out his heart.
All so he can do the deed.
I do not recognize him,
as he drags the rabbit
from its hutch
and slams it down.
Soon the animal is crucified
on the old apple tree.
My neighbour's knife unzips the skin
and with a few tugs
it is flayed, pink as a baby.
The knife now plunges deep;
guts, lungs and a small heart
drop into a bucket.
He takes down the shell of flesh and bone
and walks into the house,
past the dandelion blades
he used to harvest
for the beast.

The Midday Fox

My demon is in the garden.
Nonchalant in the noon-day sun
he bites burs from his fur
and snaps at fleas.
Not quite a fox
he grins at me in the window.
All the time by the fence
the cat watches, waits,
pretends not to care.
My demon came out of the brambles
by the skeleton of the bomb shelter;
under the ash trees
he waits for me.
The autumn sun slopes
over the rooftops;
the light collects in pools.
Over the compost heap
through the flies
my demon goes
without a backwards look.

Rainbow Over Lety*

I view from a passing coach
the broken wheel of light—
one end stuck in rutted clay,
one in forest loam.
Under the trees the leaves are flayed skin,
the roots whitened bones.
We move too fast to watch the light fade,
the dissolution of the arch into grey.
We, who are blessed with movement,
hurry past the stillness of the dead.
The restless ones rustle but cannot leave,
they for whom movement was everything.

---

* The site of the first concentration camp in Czechoslovakia, where predominantly Romani people were imprisoned.

MARK COOPER

Ground Sign*

Red clay on my shoes.
I wore them in the churchyard
with you back on Midland soil.
We slipped over approaching
the Saint's tree, one by one,
hanging black ties on its arm.
You'd have creased yourself:
our best suits slathered
in a crimson livery.
Mud climbed our bodies,
baptising us with loam.
We stepped out of the underworld
to tread your province home.

---

* Signature markings where an improvised explosive device has been buried.

KEN BABSTOCK

Meditation
after Baudelaire

Another pink one, Sadness. It'll take the edge off.
You begged for dark, dark's here now.
Toronto's under infected quilts, beginning to cough,
the gilded few quarantined, the rest of us cowed.

Our dying polis come up in purpuric welts
at all this choice, these niche markets, lifestyle's whip
ending at 5 am bent over American Standard; cults
of the last rail, Sorrow. I'll chop it up

before they come. Drip drip. The dead years
gag in knockoff labels from a 19th-floor terrace.
You can smile like a ferret but you're blind, submerged.

A bled-out sun face down in the underpass.
Non-night, in its ferraiolo or gas cape back from two tours
—gurgling, pleural, O Love, listen—arrives as an urge.

False Ecology

Lamplighter. She'd built a candle-powered convection heater
from graduated terracotta pots, bolt clamps, a bread
pan, and beach pebble spacers. I lived in dread
of ever being cold. Thus the layers, the windcheater.

Hexi Telly

Lampfire, Fuelghost, when will I see you again?

What is it you see when you look?

Bipedal form in contour, poppy fields.
Night vision graffiti greening the walls. A Chinook.

Any flame like mine, then, would do.
Any blue.

In the Brecon Beacons, before being badged, I emptied
my life into—

I've four hours remaining. The scattering can be
a stand-in.
It happens above you.

I remember the scattering, the trying to blend in.

These pictures you conjure while looking,
they're strange?

Strange if human-on-human is strange. I held up a head.

Like a lantern, as in Dante.

Like an apple or torch, as in Goya. I was a boy, once.

That is gone. That's all gone.
What's left?

Interrogation. Pattern. False gods. Endurance. Fraternity.

So take me with you into the desert
of civility.

Note

Seeing these three poems together I'm only now noticing each contains its own weak light source. The 'bled-out sun' in 'Meditation', the 'candle-powered convection heater' in 'False Ecology', and the unnamed Hexamine cooker given voice and sentience in 'Hexi Telly'. I'm a little perplexed how this escaped me—but then, poems often know more than we do, and certainly know more of themselves than their author. I could entertain my inner mystic and call this trio Brief Prayers for a Dying Sun, but I work at demystifying my own mind so hang back. And couldn't some chain of material object give an equal clue to relatedness? Infected quilts, terracotta pots, poppy fields. Appearance is mystery enough.

These were composed at distant intervals, with varying (ostensible) subjects in mind. 'Meditation' was a deliberate check-in with Baudelaire a full 161 years after *Les Fluers du mal*. The modern metropolis, drugs, loneliness, and an ill-defined nostalgia whose effects might more closely resemble anxiety. Turns out Charles got it very right the first time around. I have, in the past, transposed Pier Paolo Pasolini to present day Toronto and thought it couldn't hurt to look at a Baudelaire sonnet. It did.

In 'False Ecology', I remember consciously wanting to confront a failed marriage, the frightening, submerged currency of the unspoken that can rot any human relationship by virtue of silence and recurrence. Also, though the relationship took up more than a decade, I wanted very much to know what four lines could do about that. Short poems are as difficult as long relationships.

'Hexi Telly', to be honest, came from a Twitter acquaintance. A lovely, brilliant, humane, funny man who happens to be ex-SAS. I cannot imagine what sort of will it would take to 'return' after having been in hell. Back to 'prayer'. Poetry shares structural features with prayer: it's a vertical calling out toward an absent presence. It involves the hands, heart, mouth, and mind.

Ken Babstock

What is the opposite of an exodus?

Be honest.

Sometimes we press our fingers
Underneath the other side of our lives
Out of boredom.

When our parents catch us,

They forget to punish us.
How do you punish in the language that was brought to your mouth?

the words
themselves
are still shy.

A river language
Floats on my tongue,
Tells me lies
About myself.

It takes years until I stop
Letting myself
Choose language the way a carpenter chooses tools.

This
collective grieving or
collective memory

learns to pack in the dark, learns to love
the moonlight, learns
To travel
better without the leaven, leaves the land with
whoever's history we took in haste and still take with us.

*

I comb through my mother's hair
Like it is my own duty,
Carve out
The flow of the river
As I part with my fingers.

I make myself make
A perfect line
On her deep brown scalp.
I lose it
And make myself
Trace it back again

                         and again

Obediently.

               *

My mother falls asleep rocking a river-sized child.
There is little to say about the child
Except maybe that it cries
At the sound of its own running water.

It is afraid of waking up empty.
My mother falls asleep,
Dreams of all the children
She has birthed in-between us
In secret.
She wakes up holding a river-sized child each morning.

Creation Myth

i.

The globe is a belly: swelling,
sweltering, labouring. We are
still waiting for its waters to
break. Any day now. Any day
now. Any —

ii.

If you swallow an apple pip,
you will give birth to wooden babies
with fingers twisting to twigs.

iii.

When I was 12 my Head of Year sat me down and said
I had a special bedroom within me but that all well-bred
young ladies waited to be wed before a baby slept inside
us for nine months. This bedroom spring-cleans itself,
she said, every month the soft bedding is shed, and for
those times when we bled there were pads. I asked if she
had kids, but her special bedroom had never been blessed,
she said, a shake of the head, and I wondered but dared
not ask, what came first: the bedroom or the bed?

iv.

Ancient Egyptians worshipped Nuit as mother
of the sky. Every night she swallowed sun god, Ra:
gestated and rebirthed him each new morning.

v.

Sometimes I talk to the babies
I could not have. They ignore me
but I know they hear, in the blue
light of the bedside alarm clock.

vi.

I often wonder about that snake, how
little it would take to entice me to bite
the apple.

vii.

Why do you have no children? I'm asked. *You'd make a lovely mum,*
I'm told. But I know this is a myth: that I am empty, sterile, and cold.

Abegail Morley

Neap Tide

Someone told me children are plentiful, can be collected
like shells. I imagine their beach; a shelf of fragments,
I pile them high and underline my act in sand

so the sea folds in and fills the gaps. I hoe a trench so water
scarifies sand, tilts on the leeside and your net fills itself
with weed and somewhere in it something moves.

I watch you dance in sunlight, toss your curls and limbs
until every bit of you aches, I watch how you weigh the wind
on your chapped lips, bear its salted pain on scabbed knees.

Sometimes I only seem to watch your pain outlined
by the headland, windbreakers, the extremities of a rockpool.
None of this makes you exist.

I find a stretch of sea, driftwood, an old coil of rope
and stack it up, so you can play with it later,
                                          when the tide draws out.

SHAUN HILL

effervescent

the person dying of cancer is portrayed as robbed
of all capacities of self-transcendence, humiliated
by fear and agony
                            Susan Sontag

at the fuzzy edge
of morning: morphine

your veins flood with the feeling,

their worn-out elastic
unwinding, widening—

they release you of this weight.

as you lie back to lift
a lake from your legs.

tough woman. you endured this

plump sponge of a life I think
you're ready now to squeeze—

wake up little nanny,

your daughters are outside.
they've come to crouch here

cup your neck, wet your hair

the curve of air
        beneath a capsized boat.
                the blossoming of new
                        blood inside a backbone.

a shoal of fish fizzing
        up into foreverness. space
                suit spinning out into
                        deep, deep stillness.

just listen to those clouds
        decork their applause
                as you lie full & peaceful
                        as a paddling pool in autumn.

Tess Jolly

The Cave

Each cry from the mothers calling their sons
back to the mouth of the cave

circles on the rim of a bowl that sings
of stars burning out in the echoing dark

but the jungle sighs *not now   not yet*
as the mountain closes its fist

and deep in the stitched-up rock the piper
laughs at the mothers calling their babes

back from the heart of the woods
back from the brambled tower and the belly

of the wolf back from the moonlit door
cradling blocks of clay and lumps of wax

they howl their children's names
through the fabled columns and flames

what else would you do but beg
when the devil is restless, remembers the pact?

Darling—

I'd fold myself into you like the wet
ingredients into the dry if only you'd stop
sowing seeds into parallel lines and could

you slice the carrots into batons not discs,
refrain from slapping your plectrums
all over the rug like an army of petulant

frogs croaking those mournful chords
to which I assume you're jamming
me out of your mind like excess baggage

while mastering the art of not giving a fuck.
If only you hadn't fattened me up
on lies and fermentation: you know

how careful I am about what enters
my body, my inner dialogue is so
exquisitely critical, like picking a scab,

and our invisible illnesses keep letting go
of their outlines, blighting the corridors
with roadkill. This morning I was reading

that thing you posted on Facebook about
anxiety being the fallout of a greedy mind
when the sound of riffing insects

shifted to a minor key, a thorax snagged
in the webs of hair and flakes of skin
that clutter up our window-ledge.

Determined to be kind I sprayed the fly
to death and wiped away the corpse
then did the spider in too, enthroned

in its palace, busby hat glossy with longing,
stomach sucking on cake-envy. Darling
I'll concede there's nothing more you can say.

COLIN BANCROFT

Bedroom Cupboard

How easy is a bush supposed a bear!

Theseus, *Midsummer Night's Dream*

During the day it is a treasure chest;
Packed tight with shirts, coats, trousers, skirts, dresses.
Clothes railed to the right, a waiting queue.
On the floor footwear; boots, trainers, smart shoes,
Stand emptily. Boxes of documents
Wedged on shelves; case files on the occupants

Lives. When the door is open it shows just
Enough to catch the eye. Beguiling lust,
Inviting a quick rummage among the frills
And laces, leathers and wools. Tactile thrill,
Not knowing what secrets, what stashed pieces
Are hidden amongst the folds and creases.

But waking, in the middle of the night,
To a silent room, the moon's swallowed light,
The dark outline of the cupboard's chasm gapes.
The shadow of some unknown stranger waits,
Standing, as deep and black as a new cut grave,
Where nothing is ever stacked, railed, racked or saved.

Leila Howl

Tides

Where is it that you linger?
Nereids hunting urchins like fingers drinking dusty spines.

Where is it that you loiter?
Sun-basked carp from benthic realms—heady and replete.

Where is it that you dawdle?
Drawn through lapping tides to paint the earth with ripples of sand.

Find it and stay there—
shed those shattered scales and lie naked in the sand,
at peace with every idle wave that washed you to this land.

MARIAH WHELAN

Four Deaths

I.

There is a hole in my thigh, a scratched mosquito bite filled with hard, clear resin. It is the summer my grandparents die. I sit in my aunt's house watching *The Simpsons* on her enormous television and pick at the skin that rings the bite.

I don't know yet that this is what happens after death: the smell of polish in an empty house, sunlight coming through the blinds.

I hold the plug of resin to the sun.

II.

I come to understand if you are young enough, you can come back. My brother is twenty when he falls into death up to his neck. The surgeons work in two teams to pull him out and when he wakes up he is eight again.

My mum prays the glorious mysteries by the light of the nurse's station. My aunty explains to me what a synapse is.

When he comes home, my brother sits in the dark dining-room holding his head and resting his eyes from the light.

Twenty-five years later, he stands by the kitchen door at mum's smoking roll-ups. He tells me about a rule change to this year's rugby.

I say, 'Oh right, why's that then?'

It is not the first time he has told me this. I know he will tell me again.

III.

My uncle dies next—the hospital forgets to give him his insulin. Because I'm old enough now, I go to the funeral. I have been obsessively reading and re-reading *The Secret Garden*. I spend a lot of time outdoors and ask my mum for a beret. I wear the beret to the funeral and I know this is true because I can see it in my hands—I can feel it in my hands as I roll the wool back and forth. And the church floor behind my hands is a smear and my aunt's face behind the coffin is a used up scratch-card and I can't look up from the blue wool between my fingers because I can't look through the scraped-off afternoon to where her face should be. I know this. I know.

IV.

Although he is the eldest child, my dad doesn't give the eulogy. What would he say? He smoked a pack of Superking Blacks a day, did not drink water, did not exercise except to walk to the shop for more cigarettes. How he ate cereal and toast for breakfast and had a slice of angel cake for lunch. That he was seventy-nine.

We arrive forty minutes early for the funeral but stay in the car, parked around the corner.

'Give it a minute,' he says.

Fossils

Once there is nothing left to dream
they fill my sleep: the cold weight
of his mud-stones and shale, a stalagmite
pale and thick as a baby's arm.

And when they come he follows
in his moleskin coat, dragging his boots
through the frothing water, bending
to shuck and peel back the turf.

Here is my dad climbing into my dreams
with a torch between his teeth—
he presses his hands into the crumbling wall,
lifts a single slice of oakstone to the light.

He's left me no notes, no name plates
to show me where he found these stones.
I keep them in a box behind the sofa,
lay geological charts over his ordnance surveys

but I cannot make the fault lines match,
even walking through his village in dreams
to the moorland he spent years searching
for that one perfect specimen.

In the morning, I will walk through my estate
pocketing melted glass and concrete,
stuff bits of brick into a carrier bag
like a magpie studs her nest with silver—

gum wrappers and cellophane,
things she doesn't understand
but thinks beautiful.

Rhiannon Fidler

Sacculina

Your larva found my skin when the tide was at its highest:
with lips lazied by saltwater, your meandering tongue
danced loosely on my neck as I shook off my shell,
my exoskeleton replaced with mistaken familiarity.

You punctured my flesh with keen fingers, clawed deeper,
unhatched a fondness thought to have been lost
as your cries in the night replaced the blood in my veins;
you penetrated my thorax and took root in my heart.

Sacculina, the depths of your ocean know no bounds,
but in idle moments I have taken to searching
for a semblance of the glow you sought out in my skull,
before it seeped into every crevice and spoiled from within.

How I craved you in the morning, yet found the waves silent and still,
circled every syllable spoken, showered as if to shed my muted moult,
while you skulked in the shallows, eager lips lazy upon another.
I mused on your distance, resolved that you were captured in the drift.

Milena Williamson

Ill Met by Moonlight

[Enter, from one side, BRIDGET CLEARY, with her train;
from the other, MICHAEL CLEARY, with his]

Fairies, skip hence: find me an herb
to charm his sight and make him madly
dote upon a creature. I will be
the next thing he waking looks upon.

Women—you will know a man
by the garments he has on—
streak his eyes so he may prove
full fantasy or more fond of me.

He makes me the breathless housewife
by never giving me a drop of milk.
I will never let the stains out of his clothes.
I dress in weeds wide enough to wrap a fairy in.

Badger the Dog

A handkerchief falls to the floor—
the first remembrance from her husband,
BRIDGET CLEARY reserves it evermore about her.

Her feathered hat hangs in the bedroom
and an earring glints in the ashes.
He scrapes off the juice of some creature.

I follow the scent to a shallow hole, to my lady.
The peelers arrive and place her body
in the outhouse to mask the smell.

I guard the outhouse like the gates of hell.
I lie in the dung and there's not a woman
who comes up the road who could be her.

Intermission

[BRIDGET CLEARY exits with the audience and finds herself in another era. She follows a group of women who are discussing lace underthings: how could they call that evidence. Fuck's sake. Total shite. Tell me about it, BRIDGET says. Everyone stops talking and looks at her. The sergeant found my nightdress when he climbed through my window at night. He picked the lock and wrote all down: such pictures, the adornment of my bed, the contents of the story, what I had been reading late. They held up the nightdress in court as proof. The woman with the mole asks, proof of what exactly and BRIDGET can't remember, as if she were asleep when it happened. The woman touches BRIDGET's arm, a motherly touch.]

Note

The three poems presented here are taken from a pamphlet about Bridget Cleary. The project, which is yet to be published, was supported with an award from the Arts Council of Northern Ireland. Bridget was born in 1869 in County Tipperary and was an unusually independent woman. She attended school and earned an income as a milliner. At twenty-six, after a long illness, she was burned to death by her family because they believed she was a fairy-changeling. Among the many changeling-burning cases in Ireland, Bridget Cleary is the only adult victim.

Although her family members presented conflicting narratives of the events leading up to her death, those who played the most active roles were her husband Michael, her father, and two male cousins. I use 'role' because identity, or the performance of identity, is central to my work. The poems alternate between Bridget's perspective and her family members' perspectives, investigating why some identities are viewed as more dangerous than others.

The judge at the trial of Bridget's family said, 'We are not here acting a play, but to inquire into matters of fact.' Yet he also quoted from *Macbeth* to describe Bridget's untimely death. My poetry illuminates the Shakespearean nature of this case. What if the herbs Bridget took for pneumonia were the love-sickness ones from *A Midsummer Night's Dream* that make a man 'madly / dote upon a creature'? How does Bridget's handkerchief, a gift from Michael—which parallels Desdemona's own from Othello—shift from a token of love to proof of murder?

'Intermission' breaks the fourth wall that is the play of Bridget's life. Bridget overhears women discussing the acquittal of a man accused of rape, a case that took place in Cork in November 2018. The women discuss 'that evidence', the despicable use of a seventeen-year-old's lace underwear as proof of her consent. Bridget misunderstands the contemporary context and reveals that her underwear was also held up in court—as evidence of her murder.

The Shakespearean references in these poems, as well as my project's three-act structure, attempt to refute the judge's claim. In Bridget's life and death, in which identities are constructed and belief overpowers evidence, we *are* 'here acting a play'.

Milena Williamson

The local historian questions her life

Gather up the fragments so nothing shall be lost.
John, 6:12, motto of the Federation of Old Cornwall Societies

At weekends she crawls tips
        for the last of the tape players.
                She can un-jam all the photocopiers
                        in all the reference libraries
                                for fifty miles.

                                Once she loved a man who wrote the future
                                of paper: all the ways to weft it, have it burn.

Her days are laid out
        in the tight column inches
                of long-gone county dailies.
                        She dreams in acetate.

                                They holidayed in new countries
                        where the recent past was bloody.
                There were no records of those trips.

She cashes in her pension
        to save an archive of timetables
                of forgotten bus routes.

                                That man who wrote the future
                        left for someone who knew nothing
                of tithe maps, was keen on recycling.
        Her letters got emailed replies.

She gives her best years
    to the back rooms of chapels.

              Who's alone while the dead clamour
          to be gathered in from damp
      parish rolls, bills of sale?
    Who's alone? she asks the box files
in the night. Who's alone but me?

CLARE CROSSMAN

Bird Watching

It's a joy to be hidden, but a disaster not to be found.

Winnicott

The walls you painted years ago are enough
for you. White, and a Chinese screen
provides colour. You live plainly
and know that when you look out
of the kitchen window to the roofs
there will be no one at your shoulder.

When you come home, after a day of listening
to other people's stories, everything
is as you left it. The unwashed plate,
the novel you are reading, fraught messages
caught in the answer phone, until you listen.

You like alone. The clarity of it.
A rhythm, punctuating your days.
The walk to the tube for work
and the contemplation of what's been
hidden. Starlings and pigeons
flock above your head.

In high summer you follow them
to wagtails, oystercatchers, swallows
on the sweep of Norfolk marshes.
Thinking on those you love
on the sharp rising of their curves
and tilt of wings.

They define the air as they wish.
Put aside the pavements,
the rush, the get and spend.
Defying everything that pins us down.

JACK COOPER

Exposed

A boy still, on this beach.
Skies smooth as fitted sheets.
Seas blue and foaming, thick
as laundry detergent.

Mum lays out sandwiches,
rubs suncream on my back.
She's so kind, but I wish she wasn't
where the older boys can see her.

Those boys—all bite and bravado,
playing rough in the sand.
I watch, pretending not to.
One is running from the rest;
taut and tan, wasp sleek,
laughing a little too loud.

And they have him pinned,
trunks jerked down to black rough,
that soft tumble.

Mum calls but I am already turning to her,
too fast for shame to catch up to me.

DANIEL BENNETT

Where It Takes You

How far it runs. Stretching out
beyond the bedroom wall,
of the white stippled cottage:
that first road, that minor track,
a thin Rubicon to the pasture
beyond a barbed wire fence.
In summer, the tar would loosen,
running like paint under the crust,
gumming curled earthworms
like cicatrises in the pitch,
a grave to slain pheasants,
brittle frogs, tanned as jerky.
The evening light bulged
against nylon curtains,
as fast traffic unzipped itself
through the surf of that air,
although, I will often recall
the distant sound of trains,
rare night trains, bringing milk
and aggregate, singing me to sleep
with their rattle and shuck.
The road waited, carrying me out
towards the Molyneux's house,
where we rehearsed pyromania
in the dank breezeblock garage
while the mother sunbathed,
reading paperbacks that startled us
with their gruesome covers:
a mouth stuffed with pink worms,
a Buddha sprayed with blood.
The electric substation raining
daggers on its sign. The brambles
and deadly nightshade. Rat-traps
and green algae. The time I swung out
on my bike, turning into the path
of a speeding car. The first road
patted onwards, long after
I left its edges, like a lost friend
driven by obsession or loyalty
to spend years tracking me down,
slapping down its long foot,
beating its way to my door.

At The Frontier

I look back on those days with a kind of awe,
the engine in my head gone wild,
chopping up clay, foliage, nudging farm machinery
to roll loose across the landscape

down into the valley between the old hills.
The pool of mud was meat under moonlight.
Someone lit fireworks in a darkened annex.
The hooded man offered a long-toothed smile.

These things I can confirm. We built the outpost
to watch for forest fires. Corrugated iron, lichen breeding
in the dust of corroded paint. A dream of walking
under pines, of walking through cities

of walking without end across mountain paths,
sleeping where we fell. Finally we recovered the machine,
although it defied logic, its gears seized up. We became slaves
to its working, the tiresome churring and oil changes,

or we strove under the rules of old gravity,
and spent what was left of our days accommodating
the sprawl of a stranger's body, the paths backwards,
the yellow maps stuck inside our paperback books.

SHARON PHILLIPS

The Longest Day

By the time we wake it's eight o'clock
and the sun is high above the rooftop,
silvering the snail trails that spool out
fresh each morning over our back wall,

its stone blocks pitted with tool marks
and with shells from Jurassic beaches;
the light's angle picks out each flaw,
turning the blocks to reliefs of the cliff

where we walk after the phone call
with your blood test results. We blink
against the sting of sun on limestone

and stop to talk, looking down at the bay
where the foreshore is dotted with rubble
that will blaze rust red at sunset.

An astronaut dreams

that she grubs a pebble from the soil,
holds its cool weight, watches worms
wriggle through leaf-mould, a bee
nudge rosemary stamens

sealed in her pellet of metal, she hears
the ack of a crow, smells the molasses
stink of new-spread slurry, strokes
the silver fuzz on leaf buds

then dips her face to a basket of linen
fresh from the line, sees a grey feather
snagged on a rosebush, soft foliage
deep red, about to uncrinkle

she floats through the shallows of sleep,
dreams that rain pelts a window,
a snail glides up the glass, beyond it
the earth and infinite black.

GERALDINE CLARKSON

Still Life

To Brother Jacob, I bequeath my two best orchids,
severed blooms, frozen globes, capsules of distilled
desire, unfulfilled, tender hurtlings;
for him to keep in chilled lead crystal, and display
on feastdays, on split pine, in primrose late-day light,
a Dutch interior, with some must-bloomed claret grapes perhaps,
thick-waxed apples, and maybe a grinning skull: *here lies beloved*
Brother Gilde.

Book of Blue

Mid to ¾ way through a gold and crimson century,
a monk, glad from Nocturns, committed himself
to fix a thousand words, all slippery and impure
for secular posterity. His papery hands illuminated
each one with nipples, curves, and quim,
in quick strokes of a vigorous quill.

Ignoring strictures of obedience, he privately celebrated
created genitalia, praising the bawd. Acedia kicked in
at 666. Beside him, scroll after scroll of cobalt-
drenched parchment blown to brightness, rolled
high against cell walls. The great Bede himself
was piqued. And Father Abbot's eyes only
averted; dilated; watered.

Wing-broke Angel

A wing-broke angel, prone on the lemon laminate floor
of the library, stunned and starry-eyed. I admire the hulk
of the one unbroken wing rising like surf
from young unmuscled scapular bone.

A total waste of money, one Midlands matron
vents. And *Is this room all there is?*
from another punter. January sunset burns livid
against front-facing 'Spring Reads'; seraph breaths

grow sparse. The very first time
an angel has visited: no protocol to speak of.

Note

Having these three poems selected and juxtaposed by *Poetry Birmingham*'s editors has highlighted for me how certain themes of work and life experience surface regularly in my writing—the monastic/the rule of silence, and the book/library.

Public libraries were a major part of my childhood—a happy refuge for a bookwormy, story-loving girl at the lower end of a large working-class family. Later jobs in libraries, and also offices, churches, care homes, and warehouses—all curiously foregrounding similar habits/values of quiet service and conformity—both influenced and impeded my writing. I had the experience, also, of spending some years in a monastic order, which observed a strict rule of silence. In fact, a culture of silence, a kind of non-negotiable opp/supp/re/pression, was dominant until, following the shock of a major bereavement, I began to write poetry. Quite suddenly, words flooded out, urgent and unstoppable, challenging and transgressing the silence. Early publication, paradoxically, re-complicated the issue, the precious stuff retreating underground and having to be winkled out with titbits, if at all. Something to do with the brain's two-sidedness—the intuitive self versus the editing/monitoring superego... In many ways, publishing is a tantalising foil to my praxis. Pre-writing, I used to covet the freedom of visual artists to communicate directly without the prevarication of words. A quote from the artist Celia Paul resonates: 'Painting gave me freedom of speech. Gradually painting took over from the prose, the poetry and from any words at all.'

My poems often latch on to colour and the visual, as here. The 'blue' of the title 'Book of Blue' chimes also with a salacious-monastic streak in some of the poems ('quim' is slang for female genitals, and the orchids in 'Still Life' have associations with male genitalia—the name of the flower derives from Greek *orchis* meaning testicle).

'Nocturns', mentioned in 'Book of Blue', is one of the seven liturgical 'Hours' punctuating the monastic day, an external stricture aimed at cultivating inner detachment. *'Acedia'* is a monastic term for spiritual lethargy or hopelessness ('a foul darkness'), and '666', of course, is the name of the beast in the Bible's Book of Revelation.

The Rule of St Benedict, the most popular monastic rule, has an exhortation to 'keep death daily before one's eyes' and this fits with the *memento mori* tradition celebrated in 'Still Life's constructed tableau.

Medieval monks are credited with preserving European literature via their diligent copying and cherishing of manuscripts. At a time when libraries are being starved of funds and closed down, access to, and respect for, the written word is paramount. And language prefigures reality: vibrating on a mystical level, the Word becomes flesh.

Geraldine Clarkson

MARK FIDDES

Adoration and the Asp

For a century after lunch
twin pharaohs lie by the pool
on sun-beds, sprayed a gold
that wafts bergamot and cinnamon.
Their nails are white as ibises,
their eyes kohled Horus black,
cheeks chiseled, lips embalmed.
I am the hieroglyph on holiday,
sideways on to everything,
head of an eagle-cat-owl-snake.
Or Burton in a micro toga on set
before his shimmering Elizabeth
who always looked more at home
with adoration and an asp than
a Welshman with a firkin chest.
These Cleopatras also have it all,
accessories for the Afterlife:
Samsungs, atomizer, shades.
Maybe I will find them there,
me as an extra on a painted barge,
fanning them with ostrich feathers,
all of us with immortal longings,
following Ra to the field of reeds.

Another Solstice

With no virgins to sacrifice,
I spend this year's birthday in Tesco
freezer-deep in pimpled turkeys,
Bublé crooning Come All Ye Faithful
with some spillage in aisle six.
Outside, as the grey day shrivels
westwards, I receive a Firebird.
Its wings blaze across the horizon,
feathers dropping like molten gold
over tower blocks and commons.
Blinded vans pull over to the curb.
Everyone turns to capture my gift
on their phones before its flight back
to Eternity leaving ashes in our eyes.

Fiona Cartwright

Harlequins*

They gather on the glass, tapping it
with tarsal claws.
                        The crowd swells
with incomers, their elytra
scalpeled open,
                  their black wings
unfolded like hang-gliders of widows' veils.

I sit on the inside, coffee stopped
halfway to my lip
                  as I watch them probe
for imperfections,
                        their forelegs peeling
the paint of the frame's edge like apple skin,
wearing wing casings cloaked
            in the borrowed spots
of *Cocchinella* beetles, coating themselves
in any stolen colour they like.

They're not who they seem.
            The harmless ladybirds
of your childhood skulk
            politely under leaves
for winter. These polychromatic Cathys

are scratching the window
            for their Heathcliff
breaking into your home
            to squat until spring.

---

* Harlequin ladybirds are a recently introduced and invasive species in Britain. They enter
buildings in very large numbers in autumn to overwinter.

Pocket Globe, Ashmolean Museum

I want a globe
to carry in my pocket, to roll in my palm

like a lime. This one's from 1775—
too late then, for dodos

stalking across the Mauritian sands.
As I press my eye to the case

a great auk steps across
an Icelandic lava flow stilled

to stone; a spectacled cormorant squats
on an egg smaller than a microbe;

a swarm of passenger pigeons
shadows the soil like locusts.

This earth is gift-wrapped
in extinct constellations.

I can't resist.
I reach through the glass

and take the world
hand it to you, my child,

and you try to hold the birds to it
under your thumb's gravity.

LUCY CRISPIN

wormholes and paradox

The Archaeological Museum of Chania welcomes the Gods of Aptera

museum poster, summer 2019

These stick figures, metal dulled brown,
are caught in clumsy beautiful port de bras,
left arms hooped out at chest height,
right hands lifted to the forehead: venerating.
Simplicity transfigured by honesty
they ask, out across four thousand years,
the usual questions: how should we live?
what matters? is there any help out there?

In another case, Roman mourners sit in stone,
old women spread with age, sheathed in scarves,
toes peeping out from beneath their skirts.
Their eyes are cast down, faces serious,
not sad; they are simply looking at the facts.
You can see that their hands clutch closed
their shawls from the inside; that they have sat
patiently, and long. Displayed nearby,
three flattened ovals of wire, thick with verdigris
and time—one end sharpened, the other
folded back on itself to receive the point—
are instantly recognisable: nappy pins.
Connection bolts, earths at my heart.

I sit at the museum's door, looking out
over the bleaching, sun-shocked garden.
Beyond it, the noon hour café hum, the roar
and jostle of the street; within, broken-off columns
stand in grass; a stone fragment of lion;
a mantle; our lunchbox, sitting on a Roman plinth.
Behind, a step away in the dim cool quiet,
this assemblage of wormholes and paradox:
how tiny we are, and how large;
how our lives mean everything and nothing at all;
how these things have always been true.

Gleaming in the gloom, Apollo and Artemis
are marble sleek, aloof and beautiful.
In a chair at their feet a teenager sits silent,
absorbed in her phone; not yet on the lookout
for gods to welcome. I reach for a sandwich
and notice the still-bright browns of a young sparrow
lying fallen in the dusty grass at my feet.

how knowledge comes

On an unremarkable, light-grey-clouded day,
as I walked into town, on the road beside me
a small black cat was hit by a car. With only
the softest of thuds, the life was pushed out of it.
Someone (not me) got it off the road; or perhaps
it was flung clear—I can't remember now. It lay
on its side. As I watched, a pool of urine bloomed
with extraordinary swiftness from beneath
the hindquarters, turning the pale pavement dark
with the strange undramatic instantaneousness
of complete surrender. I remember knowing
for the first time that there is, unquestionably,
something which leaves when death arrives;
and that knowledge was at once terrible and beautiful,
like a hunger which was its own food.
                                    Many years later,
I sat beside a friend as she struggled towards
the end. Hers was the stony road of gradual
diminishment, of small losses eroding all
but her dignity—even through those final days
of nappies, morphine pumps, the unmistakeable
low reek of decay. In the long last hours, she turned
her attention inwards: though her eyes were open
she was looking on something else, absorbed into
the last great task ahead of her. She lay canted
awkwardly to one side, half-curled as though for birth;
she panted, her pulse a feeble syncopated dance
flailing in her throat as the tired blood retreated
and her hands became blue. I remember a graze
near her left wrist where the parchment skin was torn, scrolled,
wrinkling from her like shed clothes, or something outgrown;
and I know I was not quite sure exactly when
that wild dance had ceased. But when I became aware
that it had, *Well done*, I breathed, *well done. You've made it.*
Her hand—no longer frail, but empty—lay in mine.
Without surface-tension to hold them, pooled tears simply
spilled from her eyes, as if they were no longer needed.

Alison Lock

Unfastening

Boats rest on the mud
       of the harbour floor
              sea chains uncurl

anchors half-released
       are grip fixed
              by their denoting buoys

a black-backed gull
       circles a plastic float
              nylon ropes coil in

the motion of a bi-daily flow
       lustering a patina
              on the rocks

a palimpsest of brush strokes
       a printed script
              of sea-reeds

where I leave
       my shadow of wings
              the span of my open beak

a sedimentary snapshot
       captured in the drift
              of my unmooring

where the lee of a ripple is
       a collar of sand
              swept away in an ebb.

MICHELLE PENN

Strange weather

I never thought I'd become rain.
The body, the pond swept skyward, warm and wet and spinning
and me, plummeting to earth
landing squat, a longer jump than I could ever make alone.

> *we are a blind chorus of angels we are falling*
> *angels falling our skin waxy & green our feet webbed*
> *legs splayed we splash*
> *onto cars gardens city streets then hop away*
> *dazed by force & fervour*

**people panic
shout *plague*
they clutch bibles, collapse
to their knees**

I blink, take in this new place I've been sent,
I'm a prophet, a missionary.
Each breath passes through my skin like a psalm.

**do they think the slits
in my eyes are
the devil's work?
I too have
a heart lungs blood
I have
a voice and
call out**

> *we are angels look at our feet can't you see*
> *we are angels*

[I'm no angel, I was just minding my life, about
to tongue a fly when—]

we swim through air shower down & leap
as though to stroke the hand of god

If I'm too slippery to catch, well,
salvation isn't easily had.

we are a shiver of science a joke
on your fables we shake ourselves off scatter
to find our place in this world

House of the Exiles
after Federico García Lorca & Méret Oppenheim

Inside cells, women slide on
blood gloves, soft leather painted.

(Like cream, a country
      whips itself.)

Inside, women trace the walls.
Red arteries and blue veins, painted.

(The world: all mind-
      thieves and cardboard kings.)

One day, we'll emerge, drop our armours.
The air needs to feel us moving against it.

OLIVER COMINS

Lost in Translation

I

Who else would have had sufficient courage
to sleep between such dark sheets with you?
Why were so many summer nights lavished,
smiling at rumours beneath a yellow moon?
All our days were packed with secrets then,
which no-one would have known to know.
You practiced conjuring, obscuring wounds
with sleights of hand and scattering petals.

II

We can sense the nights are growing shorter,
but spring only begins when you start leaving
our windows open. We need to clear the air,
grown heavy with others' talk, distracting us.
Some evenings, early, my almond aficionado,
we greet each other with a slice of snow cake
and share a tulip of aged spirit. Mellow fumes
engender eloquence and dismantle inhibition.

III

Ground we knew then was firm, permitting
us to travel as we wished. This is not so now,
living without the news we need, wondering
if sleep will interrupt some portion of a night.
We have shown the children how their wings
can be kept dazzling and airworthy, like ours.
What a joy to watch them fly above the mist,
wheeling and swooping over a sleeping town!

MATT HAW

Patterns Work by Repetition & So Do I

I wanted to run away with you this morning,
as much as I wanted to take you out for falafel.

Instead I poured you filter coffee, which filled the cup
so monochromatically it was all I could do to keep my hand steady.

I wasn't always like this.

      I used to rake leaves
      in an arboretum as vast & misty
      as cinematic representations of memory.

      Days like milk poured into water.

      In the winter I mulched, forked
      my rotting heaps into tree circles.
      By summer I was back to raking.

      In the evenings I salved myself
      with films about crumpled stoics
      who don't change their lives

      they were so monochromatic

It was all I could do to keep my hand steady
as I poured you coffee until I filled the cup.

As much as I wanted to take you out for falafel
this morning, I wanted to run away with you.

The Hotel Soaps

I was down to tins, dry pulses,
that jar of pickled walnuts.
Down to sundry toiletries,
thumb-sized bottles of shampoo,
coins of soap fetched back
from weekends away.

Nothing fresh for days.
I was a ribcage
on the bathroom scales,
blued by sudsy cloud.
The house was paring me
down to a herring bone.

While the soaps seemed to grow,
while the bags of lentils
swelled, split & overflowed
their cupboards, the black
pickles divided in vinegar.
The garden went to seed.

Dandelions hauled up the flagstones.
Goosefoot sowed itself
over the neighbour's fence—
she *tut-tutted* at the midden
I'd allowed, took in her washing.
Sucking the lozenges of themselves,

the soaps seemed, in their way,
to say neglect will cleanse the neglect.

Tindane

There is no key. A wooden bolt,
lathed by use, slides home
into a hollow in the drystack.

The soul of any unlocked door says
let others come   brothers   lovers
to stone bunk succour   the bothy atop

this whisker-still coastal peak.
Chronic disrepair to chronic disrepair.
Let them believe as I that this

is for them alone. Kindling. Water
purifiers. Tobacco in a zip-lock.
Marked cairns & snipe launching

from heather, so they will know
they are there. I sleep now
on the shadow side of the mountain.

ii.

It's not a dream.
I have sent you here,
so late in December

to inhabit this silence.
As good a night
as any place. To witness

the grass fold over itself.
To listen, should the stone
have anything to say.

To see if the wind
can name every one of
your bones. For your eyes

to let light in on this
blindfolded hemisphere;
a mountain hut, within stilled,

with the blustering world
without. For none of it
to make you think

of any kind of god. Just hang
your song with the others
on the hook behind the door.

Hilary Watson

Faithful

She stands at the front step
looks up at the telegraph poles,
the electric street lights.

Sobbing children drag nannies
at the crossings. *Say it matters*,
scream the clouds. Nobody
listens to the crashing bins.

Perfect thunder. Syllables of rain.
God, I love what you do to me
at night. No more, no more.

Hallelujah

Hallelujah for the worthless 50ps.
Hallelujah for broken ankles,
downed fences, hung parliaments.
Hallelujah for the caller who never
leaves a message. Hallelujah for
insomnia, for paperwork, unopened
emails & packages never collected.
Hallelujah for beer-tacky dance
floors, & swarms of men rounding
in on dancing girls. Hallelujah for
rain days, for storms, hurricanes, for
currents that rip the roofs away, that
toss down trees on tracks, for non-
fatal motorway contact. Hallelujah
for decay undoing the seams of
stonemasonry unpicked like stitch
on mouths sewn shut. Hallelujah
for mudflats, hillocks, bulls alone &
sorrowful in fields. Hallelujah for
the deaths we never hear about,
for the atheist's funeral. Hallelujah
for the spring that never comes.
Hallelujah for illness sinking into
bones, exhaustion in vocal cords,
for lost & buried notepads churned
apart by worms. Hallelujah for
hitting back, hitting hard within the
rules. Hallelujah for the solitude.
Hallelujah for gunshots, badger
culls, kennelled hounds, pheasants.
Hallelujah Hallelujah Hallelujah,
for all our fly-tipped country roads.

FREYA JACKSON

Tuesday

the smell of acid rich rain and sunlight
and your small succulent stored in
a milk-bottle on my desk beneath
the window and your legs tangled up
in my bed inside my white coverlet
with the red stain where we spilt the soup—
don't you remember?—my arms
trembling with sickness while you called
out white rabbit; the totality
of my poetry is this: intimate but inside
jokes or jabs, ragged in parts,
charged with memory and emotion—
did you forget that nothing was real?
your body left, in the morning, like
a brief prayer against a scattered sky:
there is no god in it, you swear,
just eyes and mouths and bones and
a state of atrophy that resolves away,
or becomes concentrate, until we are
only the same quiet citizens our parents
were, waiting absently for death.

Amara Amaryah is a Birmingham-based poet and storyteller of Jamaican descent. She is a Hippodrome Young Poet and has performed at the RSC's Bright Smoke, Birmingham Literature Festival and Cosmopoética (Spain). Recent poems have appeared in the anthology *30 Synonyms for Emerging* (Verve Poetry Press, 2019).

Ken Babstock lives in Toronto with his son. He is author of five collections; most recently, *On Malice* (Coach House Books, 2014) and *Methodist Hatchet* (House of Anansi Press, 2011). He was the inaugural recipient of The Writers' Union Latner Prize for a body of work in mid-career.

Colin Bancroft lives in the North Pennines, where he is completing a PhD on Robert Frost. He was the winner of the 2016 Poets and Players Prize.

Daniel Bennett was born in Shropshire and lives in London. His poems have appeared in magazines including *The Manchester Review* and *The Stinging Fly*. His first collection *West South North, North South East* was published this summer by The High Window. He is also author of a novel, *All The Dogs* (Tindal Street, 2008).

Frances Boyle lives in Ottawa. Her most recent books are a novella, *Tower* (Fish Gotta Swim Editions, 2018) and a poetry collection *This White Nest* (Quattro Books, 2019). Her writing has appeared most recently in *The New Quarterly*, *Twist in Time Literary Magazine*, and *Queens Quarterly*.

Alison Brackenbury has won an Eric Gregory Award and a Cholmondeley Award for her poetry, and has frequently been broadcast on BBC Radio 3 and 4. *Gallop*, her Selected Poems, was published by Carcanet in 2019.

Zoe Brooks lives in Gloucestershire, where she is active in community development and fundraising for the Cheltenham Poetry Festival. Recent poems have appeared in *Prole*, *Obsessed With Pipework*, *Dreamcatcher*, and other magazines. Her long poem *Fool's Paradise* received the EPIC Award for Best Poetry Ebook 2013.

Lorraine Carey is an Irish poet and artist. Her poetry has appeared in *Poetry Ireland Review*, *Orbis*, *Poethead*, and other magazines. Her poems have been broadcast on national and local radio and her debut collection is *From Doll House Windows* (Revival Press, 2017).

Fiona Cartwright is a poet and ecologist who lives near London. Her poems have appeared in publications including *Mslexia*, *Magma*, and *The Interpreter's House*. She is the 2019 winner of the Brian Dempsey Memorial prize for a single poem. Her debut pamphlet is *Whalelight* (Dempsey and Windle, 2019).

Geraldine Clarkson lives in the West Midlands. Her poems have appeared widely in journals including *Poetry* and *The Poetry Review*. She has won a number of prizes and her second pamphlet, *Dora Incites the Sea-Scribbler to Lament* (Smith|Doorstop Books, 2016), was a Laureate's Choice.

Oliver Comins grew up in the Midlands but lives in West London. His first full collection, *Oak Fish Island*, was published by Templar Poetry in 2018. Recent work has appeared online at *London Grip* and *Wild Court*, and in print with *Coast-to-Coast-to-Coast*, *Finished Creatures* and *The Fenland Reed*.

Jack Cooper is a member of Highgate Poets. He has been longlisted in the National Poetry Competition, and published by *ASH*, *The ISIS*, and *Young Poets Network*. He is undertaking a PhD in embryonic cell migration at the University of Warwick.

Mark Cooper lives in South Devon. Recently, his poem 'Chiaroscuro' was awarded first place in the Teignmouth Poetry Competition's local prize. His poetry has appeared in *Urthona: Buddhism and the Arts*, and his most recent pamphlet is *The Chalk Path* (Landlocked Press, 2016).

Lucy Crispin is a former Poet Laureate of South Cumbria who has recently been published in *The Eildon Tree, Allegro*, and *The Blue Nib*. She works freelance for the Wordsworth Trust and as a person-centred counsellor. Her micro-pamphlet, *wish you were here*, is forthcoming from Hedgehog Press, who will also publish her pamphlet, *shades of blue*, in 2020.

Clare Crossman lives just outside Cambridge. Recently, a series of poems about her local chalkstream were included in a film called *Waterlight* about the communities around the River Mel in South Cambridgeshire. Her latest collection is *The Blue Hour* (Shoestring Press, 2017).

Sarah Doyle is currently researching a PhD in the poetics of meteorology at Birmingham City University. She is widely published and was runner-up in the Keats-Shelley Poetry Prize 2019 and highly commended in the Ginkgo Prize for Ecopoetry and the Forward Prizes 2018.

Mark Fiddes is from Northamptonshire and currently works in the UAE. His first collection is *The Rainbow Factory* (Templar Poetry, 2016). He won the Ruskin Prize (2017) and placed third in the National Poetry Competition (2018). His work has also been published in *Poetry Review*, *Magma* and *The London Magazine* among many others.

Rhiannon Fidler is a writer based in London. Her poems have appeared in *Timelines* (twentyfivefiftytwo, 2017) and *Journeys* (twentyfivefiftytwo, 2018). She has an MA in Creative Writing from Birmingham City University.

Jen Stewart Fueston lives in Colorado with her husband and two young sons. Her work has appeared in a number of journals and she is two-time finalist for the McCabe Poetry Prize. Her has published two pamphlets: *Visitations* (Finishing Line Press, 2015) and *Latch* (River Glass Books, 2019).

Rebecca Gethin has written five poetry publications and has been a Hawthornden Fellow. *Messages* (Coast to Coast to Coast, 2019) was a pamphlet competition winner this year and *Vanishings* is forthcoming from Palewell Press. She is a Poetry School tutor.

Matt Haw divides his time between Norway and the UK. He received an Eric Gregory Award in 2013 and published his first pamphlet, *Saint-Paul-de-Mausole* with Tall Lighthouse Press a year later. His work has appeared in *The Rialto*, *Long Poem Magazine* and *The London Magazine*. His next pamphlet, *Boudica*, is forthcoming from Templar Poetry.

Nicola Heaney is a Northern Irish writer and poet, based in Bristol. She spent over a decade teaching English to teenagers in Bristol/Bath and Madrid before completing an MA in Creative Writing at Bath Spa. Her work has appeared in publications such as *The North* magazine, the *Honest Ulsterman* and *Riggwelter Press*.

Shaun Hill has performed his work widely, including at festivals like UK Young Artists Takeover 2019. He is a Young Poet with the Birmingham Hippodrome and co-runs a workshop at Birmingham Buddhist Centre. His poems have previously appeared in *Magma*, *Under The Radar*, and on BBC Radio 4.

Leila Howl recently completed her MA in Creative Writing at Birmingham City University. She writes speculative ficton and poetry that explores intersections between science and literature. She is senior editor at Manaleak. com's MTGUK blog.

Freya Jackson is a poet and playwright who lives in Leeds. Her poems have appeared in magazines including *Magma*, and *The Interpreter's House*. She was one of the winners of New Writing North's 2019 New North Poets Prizes.

Tess Jolly has been widely published in UK magazines and commended or placed in several competitions. She has won the Hamish Canham Prize and the Anne Born Prize and has published two pamphlets: *Touchpapers* (Eyewear, 2016) and *Thus the Blue Hour Comes* (Indigo Dreams, 2017).

Fiona Larkin's poems were Highly Commended in the Forward Prizes 2019. Her work has featured in journals including Magma *The North*, and *Under the Radar*. She has an MA in Creative Writing from Royal Holloway, and organises multi-media poetry events with Corrupted Poetry.

Gregory Leadbetter is author of *The Fetch* (Nine Arches Press, 2016). His book *Coleridge and the Daemonic Imagination* (Palgrave Macmillan, 2011) won the University English Book Prize 2012. He is reader in literature and creative writing at Birmingham City University.

Alison Lock lives in West Yorkshire. Her most recent publication is *Revealing the Odour of Earth* (Calder Valley Press, 2017). Her poems have appeared in *Pennine Platform*, *Reliquaie*, *Off the Coast*, and others journals and anthologies.

Abegail Morley's fourth collection is *The Skin Diary* (Nine Arches Press, 2016). Her debut collection, *How to Pour Madness into a Teacup* (Cinnamon Press, 2010) was shortlisted for the Forward Prize Best First Collection. *The Unmapped Woman* is forthcoming from Nine Arches Press. She is co-editor of Against the Grain Press and editor of The Poetry Shed.

Michelle Penn is a dual US/UK national based in London. Her debut pamphlet, *Self-portrait as a diviner, failing*, won the 2018 Paper Swans Prize. Her work has appeared in *Shearsman*, *Magma*, *Butcher's Dog*, and other journals.

Sharon Phillips lives in Otley, in West Yorkshire. Her poems have been published online and in print. She won the Borderlines Poetry Competition (2017), was among the winners of the Poetry Society Members' Competition (2018), and was Highly Commended in the Bridport Prize (2019).

Katherine Stansfield grew up in Cornwall and lives in Cardiff. Her poems have appeared in *The North*, *Magma*, *Poetry Wales*, and as 'Poem of the Week' in The Guardian. Her second collection, *We Could Be Anywhere By Now*, is forthcoming with Seren. She is a Royal Literary Fund Fellow.

Matthew Stewart works in the Spanish wine trade and lives between Extremadura and West Sussex. Following two pamphlets with HappenStance Press, both now sold out, he published his first full collection, *The Knives of Villalejo* with Eyewear Books in 2017.

Laura Wainwright was born in Cardiff and lives in Newport. She is author of a book of literary criticism, *New Territories in Modernism: Anglophone Welsh Writing 1930-1949* (University of Wales Press, 2018). She was shortlisted in the Bridport Prize (2013). Her poems have been widely published in magazines.

Hilary Watson lives in Cardiff with her girlfriend. She has been a Jerwood/Arvon Mentee. Her poems have appeared in magazines such as *Poetry Wales*, *Butcher's Dog*, and *The Interpreter's House*. She was shortlisted for the Troubadour International Poetry Prize (2018).

Mariah Whelan is a poet and interdisciplinary researcher from Oxford, currently finishing her PhD at The University of Manchester. She is the author of *the love i do to you* (Eyewear, 2019) and *the rafters are still burning* (Dancing Girl Press, 2020). Her work has been shortlisted for the Aesthetica Creative Writing Award (2018) and won the AM Heath Prize (2013).

Jay Whittaker lives in Edinburgh. Her debut collection *Wristwatch* (Cinnamon Press, 2017) won the 2018 Saltire Society Scottish Poetry Book award. Her more recently published poems have appeared in *Shooter*, *The North*, *Gutter*, and *Envoi*.

Milena Williamson is from Pennsylvania. She is currently pursuing a PhD in creative writing at the Seamus Heaney Centre at Queen's University Belfast. She was the winner of the Mairtín Crawford Poetry Award in 2018. Her poetry has been published widely, including in *Magma*, and *Poetry Ireland Review*.

POETRY BIRMINGHAM
Literary Journal

NOTES

#DearPoetryBrum
@PoetryBrum

Printed in Poland
by Amazon Fulfillment
Poland Sp. z o.o., Wrocław

51322006R00061